QUITTING
TIME

QUITTING TIME

poems

PATRICK CABELLO HANSEL

atmosphere press

TABLE OF CONTENTS

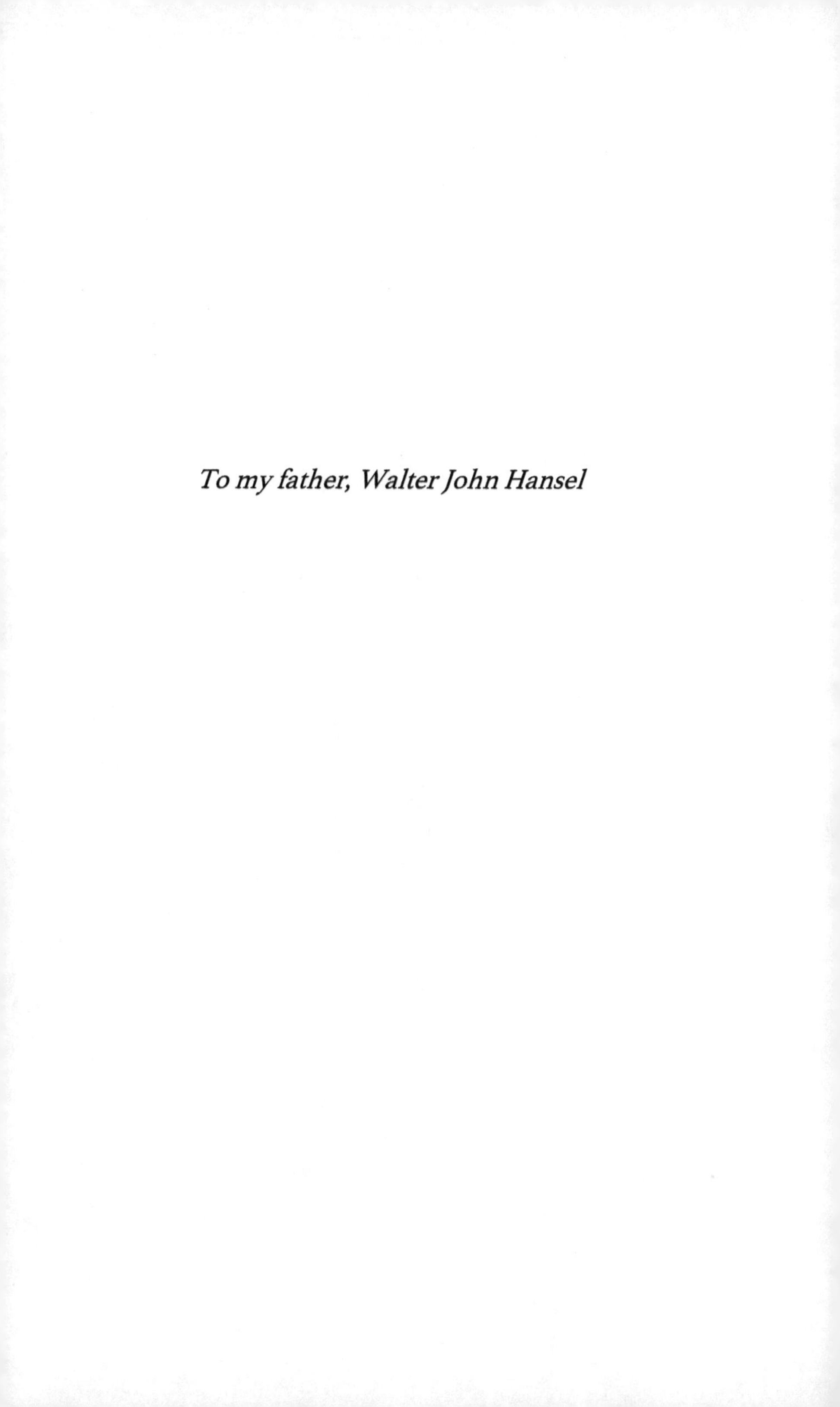

To my father, Walter John Hansel

ELEGY

> *Having lived long in time,*
> *He lives now in timelessness.*
>
> Wendell Berry

On your face, your beloved face,
your sweat skinned face, the remnant
grace of mother, father hidden there,
the wind of years, the triumphs
and the savagery, on your springtime
harvest nightfall sunlit face, let me
linger there. Let me touch it as
a baby, my fingers unfolded gently,
my voice harboring no words, let
me touch my face to your face,
Father, let us be here, face to face,
in this land we have sown and reaped,
in that time that has no wind, no
words to worry, let us touch,
Father, let us linger, let us be.

I
From This Land

Time has lost every picture of itself as a child.

Joy Ladin

GRANDFATHER, STANDING

Some thin twilights, when the meadowlarks
sang over the vast plains, he stood and stared
to the west. The sun was German, like him:
hard working, constant, to the minute
on the clock. And when the work was done,
when the hay was put up and the animals
bedded down, there was this exultation
in the western sky. For a moment,
the birds outmuscled the insects for song,
each blade of grass breathed, and
the deaths he had known, and the ones
he would face, fit closely in his hand.
Sunset twilight nightfall evening vespers dusk:

between the sky and the soil
there was this fire, watching.

FATHER, FEEDER

Early April 1918

You rise at four am, a bird stolen
from sleep. You make the sign
of the cross: forehead, shoulders,
heart. You put on overalls, shoes,
climb down stairs, grab the bucket.
You are pushing six years old.
In the western sky, the waning
moon toys with Jupiter; in the east,
the sun has begun to crawl back
from the night. Crickets hawk the air.
Sparrows gather at the burr oak tree.

First the chickens, corn and scraps,
then hay pulled down for the draught
horses, their feet puddling the dirt
floor, flanks glistening with dew.
Their bodies turn to you
for a rub, a pat, a handful
of oats offered as oblation.
You lead the milk cows to water,
then through the gate, to the small
pasture, the world they walk.

On the opposite side
of the earth, ancestors march,
guns riot, men talk and die.
But this is not your war.
Your war awaits many more turnings
of the sun; its long claw knows
your name; it will beckon. Today,
in this thin light, you have these hours
to stand at the edge of the world
alone, this food, these hands,
the words that arise from the thawing ground.

WALTER'S YOUTHFUL SONG

I remember the skies crammed with stars.
I remember the dust from wheat
and the horses coming up the way.
On summer evenings, I would lie
in the hay loft, looking out
the high west window to see
the sun paint the land with fire.

When mother had put the younger
ones to bed, she would come out
to breathe the last of the day
and call me from my perch
as you would call a nightingale
or meadowlark, without want
or trick, and she would touch

my hair, and stand with me
as the breeze lifted the land
around us. It was as if
the Lord of all had lain
down his arms, the one
that gives and the one
that takes away, and was

breath and bread and breeze
to all of us, all that moved
upon the earth, under the earth
and above it, the vast Dakota
sky a song that did not need
to be sung, but to be heard,
to be held in our arms and
in our mouths, sweet and tender.

MOTHER TONGUE

1917 was a bad year
to go to kindergarten
in Langdon, North Dakota
speaking only German.
Our father told us
the teacher threatened
with the back of the hand
each "ja" or "nein" that slipped
from little lips.
The children sat in wooden rows
and listened to the tick of time
fall from her teeth as half
a world away, blood was spilled
over ground that all claimed
and no man held.

Imagine that five-year-old,
uncertain in his farm pants
and the best shoes of the family,
playing in the dirt
outside the schoolhouse,
carving the alphabet with a stick,
making his sagas out of dust.
Then the three claps
calling the children into lines.
He wipes his palms on the air;
he looks forward to wisdom.

What do you say
when you are five years old
and the son and grandson of the enemy?
"Guten Morgen" is what his bride blue
eyes are shining, but his lips
tremble at the fear of the Lord
incarnate in an American Fraulein
whose brother is being shot at

over the ocean, and over dirt
that holds no man's claim.
She has stern knowledge
of how the world should turn
and which children should laugh.
She has standards in her hands.
But this child has no way to distinguish
"yes" from "guess"
or "passed" from "pest".
He is an unwelcome guest
in the land and county of his birth.
Watch him, as history's slow march
tramps the ground: how he tries to wrap
his synapses and the sinews of his mouth
around the new tongue and the dirt
it was born out of.
Watch his tongue.
Watch his hand.

THE SECOND BREAKFAST, 1924

Bacon, pancakes, ham.
Fried eggs, sweet bread, milk.
The women brought coffee
in steaming pots, wild berries in thick
bowls, sugar, a tablecloth
to spread about the harvest field.
Men and boys up since five
commanding horses rightly swooned.
It was the late summer family wedding feast:
a marriage of toil and rest,
the hungry mind hailing the harvest.
Wheat, barley, oats—the ripe heads
snipped by the combine, chaff
driven to the wind, grain gathered
by hard work in silence, the winter
secured, shoes bought for half the family.

From beyond the second rise,
the cry of the harvesters:
Here comes the second breakfast!
Reins tugged back on the horses,
the combine geared down
with sputters, grace pealed from
lips for cream, butter, jam, the tongue's
delight. Your mother was still

alive at the last breakfast, bouncing
along on the hay wagon, her thick hair
streaming, the son who will burst
her kicking in the womb, his lost family
waiting beyond the horizon.
But not a whisper of the pain
on this September Saturday:
only beans, cheese, apple butter
and the cool breeze the earth
sends up to its victors.

DEPRESSION COMES EARLY

Before the banks failed, before the high
faces of Wall Street fell like burnt angels,
there was this dirt. Pounded sere
by the sun, plowed by the wind and
German men too stubborn to quit.
Each year the skin of North Dakota
was torn off, blown eastward into
the Red, the Missouri, the Minnesota,
until only the bones were left, cracked
and bereft of marrow, and whole
counties became fallow for dust.

We thought of selling the horses,
the tack and plows and moving
into town, but what demon or
damn dirt farmer would want them?

The crop prices fell, the wind
grew wilder, the cash slimmer,
the nights emptied their stars.
The Klan found easier targets:
Catholics, immigrants, those who lived
in shacks off the main railroad out of town.
Their crosses blazed at farmhouse and field.

We kept at our prayers, on our knees
after supper, and in our beds, even
as God remained hidden in a handful
of dirt, his nails bitten down to stubs.

Still, hungry mouths maw onward,
sons begin to shoulder the guilt
of fathers, families tuck their grief
into silence. War begins to call,
rumors of work in far off oil fields,
get-rich schemes with a backwards smile.

The poor shall inherit the earth,
but the earth inherits only the wind.
Every step I took burned upward
through my skin. My flesh became
home to wandering, falling, wound.

We belong to the land
we were born into only
while the land behooves us stay.
Soil turned stubborn becomes
a curse upon its inhabitants.
It will swallow its own young.

We learned to watch the birds
for hope, as if their wings
were sirens, not bedeviling us
but bringing word of rain to
the beleaguered host. Justice,
mercy, bread—the words bit our lips.

The nation made it through.
The wilds of war built factories
and God relented with the rain.
Millions moved the plains
to the coast, millions more moved
to town. The dust still rumbles.
"The farmer is the man
who feeds us all," the song said.

And the earth remembers.

THE PRICE OF WHEAT

What should wheat cost
when it's planted by a young boy
plowing behind draught horses,
while his mother lies dying
at home, the cost of her last-born
son cutting the string that binds
death to family? What should
it cost when the rain stops and
the locusts multiply and the banks
fail and all manner of hell
is unleashed upon the land?
What should its measure be
if the boy grew hard as his hands,
the father cold as a cigarette burning
in a dark, dark room, the county
falling down around itself
and the whole country following?
What wars and devastations
would rise from its restlessness?
There is bread that is made to eat
and there is bread that is made
to sorrow. Dirt, rain, seed,
hooves, time, hands, blood, fire.
Every day it is kneaded and left
to rise on the stove top; every day
we eat without remembering is
a sore on the tongue. We are
the bread. Who swallows?
Who laughs? Whose pockets?

FOR ANNA SEBASTIAN

You brought four languages
with your name and passport,
picked from the air churning
around a Europe torn over,
never forgotten even as you
whittled your tongue down to fit
America. *Erde, chleb, víz, dam.*
Earth, bread, water, blood.

With a burnt oak chest and your
memory tight as a grave stone,
you left Kalusz the year
the cemetery stopped burying,
to try your back and your will
in this new world of
osprey and buffalo,
of homesteaders and wandering
bands of railroad men, of prisons
full of money and the wishes
of beggared children.

You told my father "All my children
will go to college," but you
died after giving birth to the last
boy; and, that year, the barn
burnt down, and the man you had
married for love and for his thick
German hands tripped over the wounds
and fell into a deep well, where
sorrow and rage made love
in the darkness, each upon each.

Where do you converse now,
granddaughter of *conversos?*
Where does your spirit fall?
This air we breathe descends

back to 1907; back to farewells,
hard bread and want. I want

to call you back from my genes,
the ones that make us speak
in any tongue, the ones that look
out this morning at a leafing tree
in early spring and cry out
for a word stronger,
deeper than green.

Grandmother,
I write to you from a century
my father failed to see,
where all his children went
to grad school, where I live
with a wife and daughter born in Chile,
another daughter descended from slaves,
where no record of you
past the town of your birth
exists on-line, in a museum
or a box. Where have you
gone? Can you see that I offer you
my fingers, the dirt of city soil
under the nails, the scent
of my daughter's hair as I bless
her onto the school bus
taking her to her bilingual world:
Tierra, pan, agua, sangre.
Dirt, bread, water, blood.

WHEN YOUR MOTHER DIED

Your German spine,
coveted inheritance,
father's command to stand.
The North Dakota soil
your family grew from had not
yet suffered a decade of drought
that would scorch so many
from the land; it would have
welcomed your feet slowly
entering, the soles, the space
between each toe, the callous
grown thick at the heel
from a year of wearing boots
too small for you, yet not
big enough to pass down
to brother Joe, holding on
to your back pocket.
There is only so much welcome
in a farmyard bereft. Grief
is grief in any tongue,
but in your native stock,
standing stoic still reigned.
There must have been times
when the child you were was
slapped down, not by the man
your father became, morose
and bitter, sitting in a dark room,
smoking, but by the man
you thought had to grow
from you, a man
who could stand anything,
a man whose arms ended
at empty space, the caress
they wished for having vanished,
not into thin air, but into hard,
stubborn, unforgiving dirt.

II
Who Shall Sojourn

Caminante no hay camino,
Se hace camino al andar.
Golpe a golpe, verso a verso...

Wayfarer, there is no way,
We make the way by walking,
Blow by blow, verse by verse ...

Antonio Machado

NO COUNTRY FOR YOUNG MEN

1933, age 21

The farms failed early, the banks late;
jobs, when found, paid less than the fist
and dirt they were made of. The spring
wheat and the winter lost to bugs and hail,
family barb wired to hurt, mother still dead.
Walk, young water, walk out the door
with eyes carving a hole in your back,
turn your face to the south wind burning:
Dust Bowl, foreclosure, the Klan, railroad
dicks with the heat of sticks to the head.
The whole world waits below
your feet. You have only to swallow
your fear, your loneliness, the land
you love. Like milk from your best cow:
warmth, splash, alfalfa, rain. Ride the rails,
sleep in parched fields, CCC, the combine trail,
the army, the war, the accident: each
step another odd job taken to your self.
When you settle in, your roam is waist deep
across the river, and your mind remembers:
I thought it was joy, but I knew it was fight.

DAY WORK

Eighty pound bales hoisted onto carts,
shit shoveled out from the pig sty,
flies batted away from my face.
Every job we could find during
the Depression, everyone that took
men who didn't talk too much,
we did them all. Tore holes
in the earth so people could eat.
Shaved sheep and cut up sows.
Packed boxes with goods we could
not afford. In the Army, shot
at targets and then at people.
In the CCC, built roads, cut down
trees, planted trees, put out trees
on fire. In the freights hitching
south or west, you held onto
everything you had, especially
your wits. When sleeping in
the barn on the combine trail,
you dreamed of home. We did not
care how we smelled. We had enough
clothes to make it to Saturday.
The pay miserable, the company
undependable. But there was
a blue sky over us many days,
and an early afternoon rain
might mean a nap before supper
without losing a dollar. The wind blew
in all the seasons and the earth
did not give up. The stars
were the same all over the country.

HOME FOR THE HOMELESS, 1930

When the farm mom brought supper
out to the combiners in the barn, did you
notice her dress? Was her hair slipping
out from her bun after a long day's work
of cooking for the hired men, putting up
with the children, and putting up pickles
and preserves for the long winter? How
much did you see of your own mother,
and how much did you imagine of a wife?
The boys ate greedily after the twelve
hour day, helping themselves to stew
or potatoes from the big pot. I see you
sitting by yourself, the long loneliness
come over you again, the home you left
in silence, the house made desolate when
you were twelve and your mom passed.
Passed *away* is what they say, as if
there was a portal through the grave
or through time for her to come back,
or for you to cross over, and yet still
be among the living. You are passing
the time alone: your sisters and brothers
left at home, your hands, your back,
this dirt. You made your daily wage,
you ate your daily bread, but your daily
march? Not knowing the way, following
the roads that appeared here and then
there, following the harvest to a home
you couldn't name. Was there a prayer
in your heart that evening as you lay
down on the hay? Did it sound like a song,
the one meadowlarks sing at the fall of dusk,
calling to their mates across the wide fields?
Or was it pure and brittle: tired breath,
hunk of bread, bit of skin, something
the harvesters left behind?

RIDING THE RAILS, 1934

Boxcar after boxcar, dust unto dust,
the shriek of metal wheels on the track
scraping away the inner ear. You were
grain hauled from the harvest,
fattened hogs ready to slice.

Everyone slept with their shoes on,
hands holding a rock or blade
to guard pockets with holes.
It was not night that robbed
but hunger that subjugated the soul.

North Dakota, South Dakota, Iowa,
Nebraska, Kansas, Oklahoma, Texas:
all states stolen for the Union by war
and treaty, seven wounds, seven stars,
happy endings you couldn't reach.

We scoured rail yards for old
shoes and cigarettes that had
been abandoned. We picked
radishes on the way down,
and field corn on the way back,
roasted over oil drum fires.

There is always work
for men willing to be
underpaid. There is always
something to be picked,
something to be shoveled,
something to be broken
into pieces and hauled away.

In every town, we learned
the rounds of cinder dicks
and their batons, where Citizen's

Leagues roamed. We met Okies
fleeing west and sharecroppers
flowing north and wetbacks willing
to surrender their skin to the sun.

The economy, ground to a halt,
still ground out its faithful
bodies. America had stopped
in its tracks, but the giant wheels
kept rolling, rolling, flattening
pennies and men in its path.

All I wanted to do was touch
the ocean, but when we got
to Corpus, it wasn't my feet
that welcomed the wide water,
not even my eyes, but my hands,
dystrophied into a fist.

Hoboes loved to ride.
Men looking for work learned
to hide: their past, their ears,
even parts of their names.
Some for years, some for one
season of harvest and shame.

By the time of the war, we turned
in our shoes for boots, but we road
the same lines: Milwaukee Road,
Atchison and Topeka, Northern
and Southern Pacific. All going
one direction: to the sea, to arms,
to our bodies honored for their loss.

THE COMBINE TRAIL, 1936

In the 1930's and beyond, young men,
many of whom had lost their farms travelled
the combine trail, following the harvest.

From Enid to Hays to Broken Bow
the wheat calls: first the stem, then the leaf
in the stem, then the ripened head, rolling
golden brown across the vast belly of America.
The wheat calls to the boys sleeping in barns,
sleeping in ditches, sleeping along the long
and sodden railroads at each end of the line,
the wheat bids them rise, hop a freight
or stick out a thumb and fly, field to field,
cutting down each sheath, twenty
to forty-five acres a day, working from dawn
into the hot and dusty twilight, dreaming of water,
water, water in the short nights they slept,
with full stomachs and aching muscles.

If lucky, they left each job with a cold
roast beef sandwich and a little money
in the pocket; if not, with beer smell and
the thin taste of blood clinging to their lower lip.
Some boy would lose a hand or half his arm
to the new-fangled machines, others would
get so drunk on pay day they'd fall and crack
their heads on the one concrete
sidewalk in a forgotten small town.

There was always one more field to clip,
always a buddy to make for a day, a week
or two working the way from North Jones
in South Dakota to Sweet Briar in North,
all the way to Winnipeg, sometimes switching
to corn or beans, or tearing down a shed
or chopping wood, whatever work came up,

until the snow came, and on its heels,
the irresistible, confusing call to home:
a longing for love, a fear of touch.

The grain was trucked to silos in small towns,
moved by train to Minneapolis and Sioux City,
loaded onto barges long as city blocks,
then sent in great ships around the world
for the hungry to chew, to swallow and long for more,
while the chaff, the spent stalks lay hidden
in the pockets of the day workers, burning through
before the solstice and the next demanding year.

I wish I could have ridden along with you
for a hundred miles or a hundred days,
we could have drunk from well after well,
replenishing the Oglala aquifer with our sweat,
taking turns keeping watch for the railroad
dicks when we slept in freight cars,
we could have gotten golden brown together
as the sun harvested our pale flesh, learned
new cuss words, drank coffee from a tin
mug in the morning, shared a smoke
as the sun when down and the wheat
was laid to rest in its barns. I would
have taken your hand in the night
while you were sleeping, turned it
over gently, talked to your blisters,
read your life line long and laborious,
and laid it back upon your chest,
to rise and fall with each dusty breath.

III
At War

*Time sweats in the middle of the night
when all the other dimensions are sleeping.*

Joy Ladin

FALLING

A man hung from his parachute
like a seed softly whirligigging down,
shouting "Don't shoot—I surrender!"
in the tongue of the enemy, your first tongue.
He had no way to reach
his weapon, but the men under

you did, and in a minute—though your voice
was raised and your rank commanded
obedience—it was the county fair
in Shreveport, in Pembina, in New Ulm
and New Prague, step right up, everyone
wins a prize, the lights flashing,
the girls all giggles and bullets
and a ribbon for the man who hits the nose.

Then, silence, the head of the boy
on his chest, his body limp
in its harness, gravity doing
its work. The son of German cousins—
perhaps the grandson of your grandfather's friend—
spoiled blood over his uniform. Father,

why did you tell me this story
and not my brothers?
Your memories are like your hands:
big, calloused, open.

His boots, newly shined, pulled him
down to the earth he finally
met as a shroud, a nothing,
a home. Your men did not speak.
They held their rifles across
their chests, as if bearing sick children.

YOU ARE MY FATHER, MY SON

You are my father, my son,
today I have begotten you in war,
on the shore of Attu Island,
stabbing with bayonet the dead
Japanese, seeking to kill the live ones
hiding among the fallen flesh.

You tell me this story
thirteen summers after
your death—through my
older brother, as we talk
around photographs of war:
white shirts rolled up
to the forearm, cigarette smoke
hovering every background.

How many secrets did you hold,
and where do you hide them
now, father of spark and ash?
Your voice is like smoke I make
with my mouth on winter mornings:
molten, fleeting, sparse.
My hands are not your hands
and my fingers are not wings
and yet, each day, they seek
the same promises the earth scatters.

The ends of the earth
are now your heritage,
the islands and their kingdoms,
the land beneath all things.
You sow silence,
and wait for another to reap.

I witness this day with my hands:
your stomach turning, your young

eyes grinding down, as you
walk along the Aleutian shoreline,
turning each face over, one by one.

Bear me.

EVACUATING

All hands but essential below deck,
life jackets on, portholes covered
with black cloth, no smoking, no noise.
You leave the Aleutians with the impediments
of war: darkness, governments, skin.
No ship runs secret—the engine cranks,
hulls break the waves, the diesel smoke
and salt spray mingle for a kind of incense.
Orders tucked in breast pockets become
a holy card, the indulgence of luck.

As a young boy, the North Dakota plains
were a vast comfort, the stars
calling each eye
towards heaven. But in the clear night
of the Bering Sea, each star is an enemy
tooth, a rocket that hates your name.

Your skin tells your body how to feel:
shivering, sweating, the flesh of geese popping
up to flail a semaphore. This sea is ruled by no
one, the iron hide of the ship is a poor man's
comfort, guns but bare sticks to the night. No

atheists in foxholes, yes, but no saints in the shaking
hold: you all prayed, you all cursed in silence:
the night, the enemy, the stars on the flag
you swore to uphold, now summoning rabid fire.
Hate is the first sin obligated by fear.

A SILENCE

December 1944

It was mostly luck.
The long guns pointed,
the terrible wings,
roaring sores on the skin of the sky.
No GPS, no heat-seeking sensor
to deliver your payload; just
eyes, training, the kind of guesses
one makes when death is a series
of commandments.

They named it "ack-ack"—
To the Germans,
a bad pronunciation of *Oh my!*
to the Americans, the sound
a cartoon bird might make,
or a chicken with its head cut off,
still squawking from its voice box
racing around the barnyard,
running in no direction
except away.

Every soldier goes to war with a promise
of bone: sheath, medulla, marrow.
You look at the enemy as a wound
that has no healing in it.
Even from the ground, the faces
seem familiar, the closing of the eyes,
the hidden fever.

There is a silence after the firing
ends, a punctuation mark needing
its own sentence. A silence,
not for the boys who are dying, but for
those left behind, those who will scrape

bodies from cockpits, round up the blood-
drowned prisoners, tell stories in their sleep.
In the morning there will be rest,
cigarettes, chow. The sergeant
will hold his hand up to his cap
to block out the sun, a country boy
private will fumble through his stack
of letters, looking for a missing word.

IN THE NIGHT

You are standing
by the anti-aircraft gun
longing for a smoke
even your eyes are painted black
and your hands don't know each other
you can't talk to your buddy
leaning into his sleep
his nose drips slow
and you want
to wipe it

To whom it may concern:
there is night behind the night
that has its voice cut off
there are sounds the ear
should not hear
there is a man who will come back
with a wound in his spine
and order it around
like a blind beggar
through his days

How many boys
who grew up speaking German
in their farm homes
now launch missiles
into the cities of their distant cousins
by the symphonies of air war
bodies leave the ground
and begin the long, steep climb to heaven

To my loving family
my sister in California
my brother farming the land
my father sitting by himself
and smoking   I have seen

the end of the world
and it scorches my tongue
pray for me, now
and at the hour of my return

In the night
you stand, hands in pockets
dreaming of home, draft horses, music
one decade from my birth
and one ocean lost
to the east, the sun has begun
to peal itself back to the world
a man in a tombstone cap
speaks orders into a radio
the dark drones pass overhead
and the big guns
the ones you've given names to
open wide their terrible mouths

ONE OF HIS MEN SPEAKS

"Damn, how I hated your stride,
that suture voice, the steady
hand. You marched us
into thick woods and
sparse fields as if pure will
could conquer every bullet.
An anti-aircraft gunner's lot
is to stay still, not give fire
until the last second, stand
in the midst of hell and count.

At night, we were firing
at sounds that hadn't happened yet.
We were guessing, often
with the part of our brain
where speech is more a visitor
than a resident. We were taking
shots at metal beasts inhabited
by ghosts as young as us.

'Steady, steady' was your voice,
as if we could quiet the shaking
of the atoms in our bones, as if
the horses our hearts had become
could be reined in. And in those rare
times we scored a hit, you let us
whoop for a long moment, and then
commanded we train our sights
on the next shot, the next drop of death.

Thank you for keeping us alive, Sergeant.
Thank you for letting us smoke at dawn."

WHAT WERE THOSE DAYS, THOSE NIGHTS?

Smoking cigarettes, playing cards,
musing on when Hitler would fall,
taking bets with your men on
when you would be going back
across the vast sea You told me

that after the war, when the jeep
accident broke your back and you
lay in the British military hospital,
you rediscovered the rosary, and
said it, bead after worn bead,
to waste away the worry, the pain,
the doubt of return.

But on those cold and hot days
in France, in Germany, as the war
marched east, what were your hours?
War is hell, and war is also
boredom, loneliness, an empty
stretch of land, fingerless and gray
in the hour before the dark.

And what of those nights?
Waiting in the camouflage
that fooled few, for the hum
of desperate pilots crescendoing
to a roar, for the order to shoot
at the unseen unseeing enemy
and pray their death preceded yours.

I imagine that some nights
the skies stayed clear, and the fighters
and bombers stayed back, and as you
looked at the heavens, you saw
the same stars you had walked
under in North Dakota, the same stars

your father had left behind when he left

Germany to try his fortune, his life
in the "New World": the Big Dipper
and the Little, Cassiopeia and
Sagittarius, and to the south,
over warmer skies and softer,
Orion with his belt, standing, war-
y, hunting the heavens as you
hunted the earth.

We heard only a few stories
about those days, and fingered
the anti-aircraft shell in the upstairs
closet, but we never heard the names
of your crew, their places of birth,
the lives and times they went back to.
If you kept in touch after,
there is no evidence: no letters,
no photographs of fattening friends holding
cigarettes smoked down to the ash,
fingers singed on the last drag.

Do you see your comrades
in heaven, father? Have they lost
their wounds? Do their scars
sprinkle light across the firmament?
And are there nights, and are
there days, when a German boy,
a boy from Dusseldorf or Hamburg
or Munich floats down on his silk
parachute, bearing not a gun
but a cross, a grin, a pack of smokes,
the last half of a chocolate bar
held out to you without a word?

CONVALESCENCE

Weary of war,
weary of forgiveness,
you lie on your broken back
in a British hospital and stare
at flies landing on your sheet.
You have one hand on your rosary
twirling the decades by,
and one on your missing gun.
You would shoot yourself
out of 1945, out of Europe,
back to Cavalier County
and its morning furrows.
From the bell tower
of the army hospital,
skin rich pigeons sing.
It is their plaint you hear,
an *Ave Maria*
of gravel and feathers.
Everyone who holds
your apology
twirls a ghost
around the cupola
of the hospital chapel.
Rest, father.
One day your back
will shovel the words out.
The eyes of your dead,
the eyes yet to come,
will open like broken wings.

IV
On the Home Front

*That is why I must try to live a good and faithful life
to my last breath;
so that those who come after me do not have to start
all over again.*

Etty Hillesum

BARBER COLLEGE, MINNEAPOLIS, 1946

Your back no longer good
for farming, you went to
barber school on the GI Bill,
rented a room off the downtown
thrum, and, night after night,
rehearsed your next life.

Snip. Cut. Clip. The red crease
on your forefinger and thumb
from holding scissors all day long,
their heads unknowable lands.
Your job to harvest
the wheat and chaff a man's
scalp pushes up every fourteen
days. Sometimes, I imagined
they sculpted the word *fortnight*
to divine your hands: fort: a stone
rebuke; night: the last word before
the light goes out.

Each evening, you took off the white
coat, shook off the tin hair bits,
the tailings of gold and coal,
then walked down the back stairway
where smells of Vitalis and sweat
still mingled, a troubled marriage. You lit
a Camel and, for a moment, dwelt
in its forgiving breath. Then out
onto Washington Avenue, where winos
and streetcar bums had begun
their rounds. Did you ever
touch their hair made wild
by grief, or reach in your pocket
and hand over a quarter—your next
night's meal: two slices of bread
smothered in hot milk? I would like
to be the spoon you ate with, its tensile

wish, the way it held up straight
to your mouth, a smile invading
yours, the silence it fathered
when you laid it down on the dark oak table.

Home to you for many
months, this city running
to grab the men the war coughed
back to its lakes and streets: you hated
its lights, its velocity, its insistence
on corn and lumber and steel.

You went to barber school,
you once told me, because you didn't
know what else to do; because your fingers
were gun-locked and your eyes opened
to the distance family breeds in us.
Every day, you practiced the comb
and cut, the clippers to the neck,
the uneasy truce of the straight edge.
I wonder what your final exam was:
one crew cut, one heiney,
one fat old man going quickly bald?
Then, no more wandering, no crop chasing
or dark night shooting at enemy planes.
You had paper now, permission
to hold men's heads in your hands
for the rest of your life.

ON THE STREETCAR

Were there some Friday evenings
when you had to choose between
a quick ride home or a long walk
into a cold wind to buy an extra loaf
of bread to tide you over the long,
idle weekend? The GI bill only
went so far, and there was the rent
on the room, the tools for barber
school, food, maybe an occasional
nickel to buy the news, or a stamp
home to let them know you were alive,
if not well. You told me, more than once,
of hot milk poured over cheap bread,
your daily feast.

Or was it all a romantic dream
I've inherited of you: the poor
man in the big city, gorged with men
pouring back into the world from war?
Maybe you had enough to carouse
with your buddies at Harry's
or Sam's or whatever bars men
frequented when out of luck
or fresh into it.

When I imagine you, Father,
on your own, no longer young,
but no certain future, and stubborn
as hell, no doubt wondering
if the life you had chosen would
un-choose you, I imagine you
talking up a storm, putting
on a brave face, gutting it out
with that blessed, grim determination
you hugged as holiness. I imagine

your hands not knowing what to do
with your body, where to put
their rage and their fierce longing
for a sign. What did you read
on the ride home on the street car

after a day of cutting strange men's
heads? Or did you merely look out
the window, at old cars and new,
streetlights stung by snow,
a hurried man covering his ears
with his turned up collar, a child
who for a moment has lost
his mother, and for that moment—

a second or two—knows hell
in stranger's faces; knows
that nothing can save him.
Not work. Not schooling. Not drink.

Wave to that boy, Walter.

AUSTIN MINNESOTA

Austin, Hog-Town,
city of bent shoulders.
Maybe the hair of the men on the kill
grow more quickly over their ears,
so that you made a killing
with your scissors and clippers
and the fine hand broom that whisked
the dead hair off their shoulders.
You roomed at Maw Daly's on Main
Street, where husband Bill left each
morning to work in the plant, and
daughter Monica checked the accounts
at Kresge's and came home to work
for the house, cleaning the roomers' rooms,
stuffing the laundry through the wringer
into galvanized pots. I wonder how
often she washed your sheets, and how
much she wondered. Mom said she thought
you were ugly and stuck up when she
first met you, but something must
have caught her heart—your mustache,
the scent of pomade and powder
on your hands, your fervency at Mass.
Somehow you ended up talking, then
dancing, then walking down the aisle
at Queen of Angels, Mom's brothers
still alive, Grandpa Bill delighted to see
his daughter finally married, Grandma
Daly wondering who would clean the sheets.

WRAPPED IN AN INFANT'S SKIN

He lies on the table, his clean diaper
soft underneath, waiting for the pins

to be fastened. Father leaves just for a moment,
there is an unknown light in the room.

What does a 10-week old reach for?
A wind, softness, skin? His joy becomes

a turning, then rolling, then falling,
his skull on the unwashed floor, wrapped

in an infant's skin. His cry, one whistle
of the desert bird, unaccountable. His eyes,

rolled back and loosing. His future? Scalpels,
skull pins, strange beds in strange rooms,

nurses holding his body like bread. His name,
cut from the mouths of his parents

like the wrong tooth, bleeds through the air.

WALTER SPEAKS

Just the one cry, and I was back to the table.
I knew it was my fault, of course it was,
any fool knows that, how could I leave you
like that, just ten weeks and lying on the table,
waiting for your diaper to be pinned. Oh son,
oh blessed head, I want to hold and mend you
together. You won't cry and you won't move.
You lie there in your mother's arms, still as stone.
In your eyes, there is a long nothingness.

My mind starts—it was just a second—
—your brother fussing—on the floor
there in the den—a little baby
can't roll over—that young—how?
Who did this—it was me, it was my hand

that left you—it was just a moment—then
it began—over, over—no stopping—
the words—the voices—they never
said a word against me—but I know that

the well wishers at church, the men
who come to the shop, the doctors the nurses
the girl who checks us in at the clinic
everyone in the family even those not yet
born know it was me, it was my hand,
it was my mistake, it is now my cry . It is your
one broken life.

LET US WAIT TO SEE HOW LONG
FOR THIS TERROR TO BE FORGIVEN

There is a strangeness in our skulls, a desert
of bone we dare not touch. When a stranger
drills open the parietal bone, peels back
the dura mater, gently pulls
the hematoma free, what does he sing?

The surgeon's hands are his compassion,
and yet he spies the worst of us, the cry
locked in wounds, the end of all
words. And their beginning. His hands
refuse to mourn that which is not dead.

The infant cannot shake the hand of his savior.
He is not awakened until the skin has been sewn up
and he is wheeled down the fluorescent hallway.
The nurses will wrap him, carry him, watch him
through the night and the day and the night.
In their daydreams, they will marry him,
a smiling boy with a bald head
stitched like a family baseball.

Long after their shift has ended, long after
their own children are fed and bathed and put to bed,
the nurses will talk to each other in the underworld
of sleep. *It is an honor to have removed
his death*, they will say, holding a pillow,
running their fingers along the hidden stitch.

TO MY NEVER BORN BROTHER OR SISTER

To imagine you is to look inside
our mother, look inside death
and see you under water,
your bones tender like shoots
of new asparagus, your smile
hidden, your heart coming
to a full stop. You never

got to breathe, to hold
in your hand a ball,
a book, a rabbit or peony picked
from a neighbor's yard. My parents—
our parents—forgot to name
you, or if they did, they forgot
to tell us. You came out wrong

and they baptized you
on the kitchen table, and that
was that. You went to limbo,
we went to forgetting. I
do not know how
to address you, little one,

gene of my genes, remembrance
not remembered, false alarm
at the birthing stool. I want
to put my flailing arms around
you, and push you back, in
time, and in our mother's flesh,

and give you something, a
sword, a little stick, some talisman
to present to the face of death.

FERRIS WHEEL

Just three years past my infant fall,
three years past three surgeries at Mayo,
three years *old*, older than birth and
the death birth brings as a promise,
I was about to climb in a metal love seat
and be pulled higher than my mortal fall.
I knew of angels then, from Mass
and the morning *muezzins* of our town:
Angelus bells, hog plant whistle,
cardinal and robin, but I do not know
if I trusted them. You held my hand
and the hand of my kindergarten-
bound brother as we stood in line,
the early August evening air filled
with the scent of pronto pups, Tom
Thumb donuts, cow barns and the dust
of mown hay floating in from the west.

Or did I imagine those smells,
and need to imagine them now,
to hold what I cannot touch? I know
I did not imagine the man, hairier than any
in your shop, snapping down the metal bar
over us, hard and insufficient for flight.
You sat in the middle, Mike
on your right, me on the left, your arms
holding us into our bodies. As the wheel
shook and began to rise, you squeezed us
and yelled a "whee!" that stayed
on the air all those metallic years—
the razor strop and clippers of your
righteousness, the bank vault door
of my resistance. It was a single
note, a hope not lost. Is that the song

I heard this morning, whistling from
the barest branch of the highest
tree in our neighborhood, nearly
done with the three score and three
years of my rising, my falling, my gift
as your son, sung with eyes wide open
and arms spread out to the sun?

MY FATHERS BACKYARD

My father loosed his little boy soul
out there, his shirt off to the warmth
of spring sun, his hand hacking
the old growth down with a hoe,
his genes expressing the olive up
into his skin, the long lost descent
from Kalusz, Granada, Jerusalem.

I tagged along,
my little fingers planting
the beans. I could not space
them right—they fell too far
apart or too close. Your word,
gentle that year: *pick them up
and rebury them*, you said.
Facing east, perhaps.
Ready for the trumpet
of your hands.

I plant today in ragged rows,
beans that have passed through
scores of generations. I pray
as I push them down into earth.
I remember your hands as I go.

CUTTING AWAY

Psalm 103

It was a small shop: one barber chair,
one barber, three magazines in front
of the plate glass windows—True,
Field & Stream, America. The middle
son washed the windows every week.
The men who sat worked at the plant,
drove truck, drilled a few teeth,
sold quality suits, used cars and cuts
of meat, painted houses, stole.
You can learn a lot by holding
a man's head in one hand
and a razor in another. The sins
dripped out of the stories they told
like honey. Most were used to a kind
of confession in darkness—a voice
a foot away, words of repentance
as far away as the setting sun is
from its rising. Transgressions
were not erased as much as shaved
down by prayers mumbled in the back
pew. But here, at Walt's Barber Shop,
each hair and the trespasses it pulled at
fell like pigeon feathers to the floor,
like rain, like wafers sprinkled in
coriander. No bloodletting in this
20th of centuries, no guarding of anger
forever. The hairs—like our sins—
were not held against us but swept
away at the end of the day, the brown
and red and gold alike. We were not
saved by the pain of our cutting, but
by its graceful release. All that was
needed was faith—simple, humble,
kind—like the seed of the mustard,

or the gel that made the front of a crew
cut stand up straight: a blessing that drew
the eye only towards the newly made face.

AT THE MANGER

"Jesus was born dirt poor," you said
and then you hauled in the dirt.
Built a Judean hillside from chicken
wire and paper maché, painted
the dark hills and red clay flats,
poured in good, black soil and
planted corn and grass seed
to grow by the south window.
We were allowed to put one straw in
the manger for each good deed done.
We were allowed to wait.

Your hands, calloused by work
and war and wandering, knew
how to build. Knew how to dig
the soul out of dirt, and what to bury.
How to curl around a cigarette,
a rosary, the razor strop.

Wounds are blessed
by the snow; the wind calling
the way away, the way home.
Maybe you prayed in silence
some Advent nights, sitting
by the one blue light in Jesus'
cave, wondering where your
life had gone, what still needed
to be born. Maybe you wept.

I don't know.

I have inherited your eyes,
your loneliness like a foreign
tongue, your fear of dying.

Each day, we moved the Magi

on their camels closer to the crib;
under the "good" furniture, past
the hot air register, chasing
a star only they could see; and
on our little living room hill, dirt
begat the common miracle:
seeds die and bear fruit,
and so do saviors. There

is mystery to that, there
is science, but finally
there is no answer.
There are songs, Father.
There is always this dirt.
My hands are like Magi
returning by another route:
empty, promising, still.

MAYBE

Maybe you should have kept drinking
all through my childhood and my escape.
Maybe a bender now and then would
have let the rabid out, and bought some
time before the next belt. You owned
your razor strops for your shop;
knew how to use them. Leather
sharpens steel, but it loosens flesh
underneath the skin. All I could
shout was *No! No!* But what you
wanted was *Yes! Yes!*— *yes* to my
weakness, *yes* to my fault, *yes* to the right-
ness of you being you. Maybe you should
have had a drink before the lesson—your aim might
have been wilder, the fire in your eyes sweeter.
A boy will learn tenderness from your hand.
A boy will learn hate. Maybe we could have
sat down together just once without fear,
your justice a bit blurry, a scent of lost home
troubling your eyes. Maybe then we might
have been able to talk during those long
teen years. But, maybe you
should stay dead until I write this.

WORK TOGETHER WORK APART

It is July, a long Friday night
and we are sweating in this tiny place
where sweat is washed off. We
bust in half the sheet of fancy
board bending it to fit around
the bathtub, and my father
swears and hurls the claw
hammer at the bathroom door,
tearing a slash in its thick enamel white.

He asks my opinion on the next try,
and I give it—a wrong one—but
one so blessed by his asking,

and as we grunt and shimmy
the board into the molding, we bump
our bodies into the porcelain tub
and each other, and I rejoice
that my father, too, can get so angry
at a thing not bending, an anger
that begs no response, and offers
no explanation, and as we struggle
over the evening's work, I think,
how cool is that, my father;
how lonely and how fierce.

I SWORE THE NEXT TIME...

I swore the next time he hit me
I was going to fucking kill him.

I held that sentence in the fist
of my chest for years, Father.

I wrote bad checks out of it.
I fell in love with the wrong kind.

I barreled my way through foe
and friend alike, hard as ice,

spinning my wheels, always alone,
leading with my nose, the bone

most often broken. And when
the thaw came, when words we had

hidden from each other began to rise,
I did not tell you this ash of hate

that still sat next to my love.
I do not want to light it

tonight, but there are days,
there are wounds.

I wonder if you still carry a match.

PLANTING YOUR GARDEN

The seed starts its first death in the air.
It rests between thumb and forefinger,
a space the mind cannot enter, but
through which hungry winds blow.
Fingers part, the seed drops, the ectoplasm
scurries to its sacrifice deep in darkness.
Big Boys, jalapeños, pickling cukes, sons:
we all die in order to grow, we all give up
our ghosts. That's what wisdom says,
but what if we inhabit our souls, rather
than them inhabiting us? What if our bodies
are not the envelopes we shrug off,
but letters written in soil, in spirit,
read over and over?

We are, no matter what we claim,
seed and egg, given and lost in darkness,
a wailing at the air, wind our first sound.

You seeded, watered, weeded, waited;
your barber hands turned to horticulture.
I see you pushing 80, taking your shirt
off, peeling off years of toil, bending to
the ground. Your smile reaches back
to a boy of five, following his mother down
the rows of the kitchen garden, planting
string beans, asking: *Here, mother? Here?*
And your mother rubs your ruffled hair,
and says the one
Russian word you remember:
dobri, dobri: my good son, my good
sower; my good boy, whom the earth loves.

RETIREMENT

Because the wandering in me never stopped.
Because the North Dakota dirt would not let go.
I was useless without my hands digging
into something. I counted five chairs
reupholstered, four walls papered, an old
TV fixed, and an older radio. I dug up
the universe of our back yard. Planted
by the moon and by the sun. Now where

do I go? Where can my name find me?

I have muscles in my mouth
that have not grown old. I have ears
soft as a sparrow's belly. I will sit
in my recliner. I will listen to the rain
furrow the hard earth. I will
release like pollen blown by the wind.
Come, earth; come stars, come children;
there is time to retune my words. Twenty two
more years, woven out of sticks and mud,
like the new nest of the robin, returning.

V
Quitting Time

I have spread my dreams under your feet;
Tread softly because you tread on my dreams.

W. B. Yeats

WHAT SHALL WE HOLD?

At the end,
all you could taste
was onion
in scrambled eggs,
no black coffee,
no radishes picked
by your own hand.
In the dining room, your recliner
became your bed, your life,
as rumpled lungs wrestled
with whatever oxygen
made it through.
On Ascension Sunday,
we gathered together
to ask your blessing
for the last time.
What shall we hold?
Words will stumble over themselves
as the years pass by,
as the ground refuses to burst open.
Who will know
your name, the weight
of your walk,
how you spoke
in rage and in love,
how you did not
take your last breath
but gave it,
the air holding your flesh,
a Pieta of wind, the last wound
sweeter, more bitter, than the first?

YOUR LAST CHAIR

As the cancer advanced through
the homeland of your body,
you settled into the lounger
that became your linen,
your perfume, your skin.
Mom brought you scrambled
eggs with onions, my brothers
and Tom helped you to
the portable toilet near the TV.
I waited from Philadelphia.

Then you stopped eating,
and stopped going to the bathroom
as you settled into dying
that was now only yours.
You did not
come to the phone when I called.
You did not answer.

I still have questions, Father.
What thoughts found solace
in your silence? Did you dream
of Anna, singing in Russian
as she lay you down, did you
smell the fields, or the smoke
of the war, did your back ache
as it let go of the long days snipping
hair in that two-chair shop of yours?

Were your words wrapped in swaddling clothes?

They say when death strikes, suddenly
our life flashes before our eyes;
but when death arrives slow—I will not
say peaceful, I will never say peaceful—

what do we see? Is the final closing

akin to the first opening—a shock
that grew into love with each breath;
or is it a slow, steady loss
of all that you held dear, all
that you were in your body and in your name?
Tell me, Father. I know you
have words you did not use up.
I know you have stories. Somewhere,
in a fallen rain, in a dust storm
or star, you must have a voice.
It is time to talk.
I can see your eyes opening.
I can hear you walking towards me.

AT THE END OF THE LINE

It was the last call.
Expected, wanted, feared.
The oxygen tank cannot work
forever. Forever does not happen
in the flesh. Your daughter
said *good timing*, the hospice
nurse *said this could be it*,
and as we prayed your favorite
prayer—the one full of grace—
you gave your last breath;
and I, on the other end
of a thousand miles of air,
kept praying, your will be done,
your life undone, forever
and ever. No more words.
Not yet the amen.

FINAL WISHES

I would have buried you whole
face up, hands folded over, snug
in a wooden box, on a farm somewhere;
not the one you had sweated
over, following the draught horses
through the dust storm heat;
nor a field combined by you
in your early twenties, the wages
you earned barely enough to keep
you in smokes and save a little
for your little sister's school
once you made the long trek north;
but a lush green field of clover
or timothy, cut up, baled and hauled
into the hayloft by boys as proud
and stupid and sunburned as me.

But you chose to be burned to ash,
in your suit, and the piece of whatever
they slid you on into the oven.
It was as if your flesh
paid for it sins twice: once with the wages
of death; the next rendered to
smoke and ash by fire too hot
to touch. All the water and land
burned out of you. We buried

your ashes in the plot you had paid
for, and, eight years later, mom's
as well. The creek that runs
by Calvary floods nearly every spring,
and I imagine that some of it
seeps through the ground
into the calcium and iron and phosphorous
that is remnant of you. *Does the dew
refresh? Can you bind your wing*

to its word? I wanted, father,
to know that something was left:
a bone leached by groundwater
and microbed down to a hard, gray thrust,
something an archeologist could scour;
something a child could uncover
digging mushrooms in the spring;
something I can hold onto , yelling

when the great flood comes; something
to pound on the earth, to make
all the dust jump.

I FEEL YOUR HANDS

I feel your hands
turning the dirt in me,

spade and long fork,
compost and new seed.

Everything you planted
has sprouted full, but

there is a scythe
waiting for us, a time

and half a time,
the long beak of

a hummingbird,
bent down to the nectar.

The furrows made
by our years grow

row upon row,
fruit upon fruit,

the bend of sore knees,
the slowing of sight.

Who will be the first
of your children

to fall, father,
into whatever heaven

holds your ashes?
I feel your hands

waiting to welcome
seeds that have not

been loosed, these bones
that creak, this earth

you bequeathed us,
fertile and full.

SEEDING

There are the shoes my father wore—
the size twelves I was ashamed of,
the white socks that glared from
the dull black oxfords. I nailed
them to the wall above the rake
and the half-eaten bag of cow manure.
Their toes point up, as if walking
to heaven is as simple as left—
right—left, the soldier's march,
the long grip on the rifle, the smokes,
the eyes never resting.

There are the gloves he wore
as he pushed the spade in on the first
warm day of spring: the crust
of moldering leaf and soot, the skin
shed by all living things. Here is
his trowel, his hallock and his long-toothed fork.
Here is the wind, ready to sow and to reap.
Here the seed I am, the seed I will never be,
and there, somewhere out there,
is his rhubarb poking its first shoots up
through the untilled soil,
the hands opening, the earth
drawn up into its verdant, crimson questions.

FATHER, DREAM

You've stopped coming to walk with me,
seeds in one hand, knife and stone
in the other, soft laments.

The twelve stones of your death
have passed through the heavens
and you've no need to water

my sleep. You are at rest.
Worms tunnel. A lone bird
sings in the early morning garden.

       Deep down,
you were Orpheus for a season,
and a time, and a morning,

calling me out of the ground,
sprinkling, pruning,
a wind I could not see. Still,

your hands hover over my head.
I wake to my own breath
shedding its skin over the wet earth.

YOU ARE IN NEARLY EVERY DAWN

You would love these cardinals
in late winter, courting from
the highest branch, the rabbits
that race the backyard snow,
sparrows who never abandon.
I sit on the porch and imagine
your face, a child I have never seen.
I have no photos of you as a boy,
no First Communion, no lost
teeth or family picnic, and yet
I see your smile as clear as wind:
a breeze that arises in the east,
messenger in a cloudless sky.

QUITTING TIME

I sweep up the hair that lies like pigeon's feathers
on my father's shop floor: Callahan's red
mixed with the dark Slavinskys and Knauers and Ryshavys,
and one blonde Swede who must have snuck
in just before five. His candied fleece shimmers
on top of the pile. Dad double counts the till
and snaps caps back onto brown bottles of tonic
and grunts with the weight of the day. And all the men,
who sat in the chair while he plied their heads
with scissors and razors and combs, the men
from the plant, still aching from cutting hogs
and steers into bite size pieces, the men
who smoke Camel Straights and hit their kids
because God says it's good for them and because
their hands were tied behind their backs
by fathers whose tongues were stolen from them
when they crossed the sea, all of them have
trailed off into the twilight like fog,
leaving their hair to sparkle under my broom
as my Father and I work in silence, and in hope of wings.

ACKNOWLEDGEMENTS

I want to thank the many poets who have mentored me, including Phillip Schultz, Ed Bok Lee, Bart Galle, and especially Jude Nutter and Richard Terrill, for their help with the manuscript. I am grateful to the Mower County Historical Society for their excellent archives, and to family members that shared stories with me. Finally, thanks to the writers' studios at the Loft Literary Center in Minneapolis, where much of this book was written and refined.

The following poems first appeared:

"Grandfather, Standing" (2012) and "A Silence" (2016) were published in *Passager*

"Father, Feeder" was published in *The Meadow* (2015)

"No Country For Young Men" was published in *Red Earth Review* (2014)

"Falling" was published in *The Ilanot Review* (2014)

"Wrapped In An Infant's Skin" was published in *Jack Pine Walking Stick* (2014)

"Let Us Wait to See How Long For This Terror To Be Forgiven" was published in *The Meadowland Review* (2013)

"To My Never Born Brother or Sister" was published in *Switchback* (2016)

"Cutting Away" won *Lutheran Arts' 500ᵗʰ Reformation Poetry Contest*, and was published in *Christian Century*. (2017)

"Seeding" was published in *Alalitcom,* the online journal of the *Alabama Writer's Conclave* (2012)

"Father, Dream" was published in *Rose Red Review* (2014)

"Quitting Time" was published in *Turtle Quarterly.* (2010) Nominated for a Pushcart Prize.

"Walter's Youthful Song" and "I Feel Your Hands" were published in *Crossings Center Poet-Artist Collaboration XVIII* (2019)

"In the Night" and "Convalescence" were published in *Watershed Review* (2019)

"What Shall We Hold" was published in *Twisted Vine* (2020)

"Mother Tongue" was published in *Heirlock* (2020)

"Depression Comes Early" was published in *Burningword Literary Journal* (2020)

"The Second Breakfast" was published in the Anthology *"Goodness" by Wising Up Press* (2020)

ABOUT ATMOSPHERE PRESS

Atmosphere Press is an independent, full-service publisher for excellent books in all genres and for all audiences. Learn more about what we do at atmospherepress.com.

We encourage you to check out some of Atmosphere's latest releases, which are available at Amazon.com and via order from your local bookstore:

Big Man Small Europe, poetry by Tristan Niskanen

In the Cloakroom of Proper Musings, a lyric narrative by Kristina Moriconi

Lucid_Malware.zip, poetry by Dylan Sonderman

The Unordering of Days, poetry by Jessica Palmer

It's Not About You, poetry by Daniel Casey

A Dream of Wide Water, poetry by Sharon Whitehill

Radical Dances of the Ferocious Kind, poetry by Tina Tru

The Woods Hold Us, poetry by Makani Speier-Brito

My Cemetery Friends: A Garden of Encounters at Mount Saint Mary in Queens, New York, nonfiction and poetry by Vincent J. Tomeo

Report from the Sea of Moisture, poetry by Stuart Jay Silverman

The Enemy of Everything, poetry by Michael Jones

The Stargazers, poetry by James McKee

The Pretend Life, poetry by Michelle Brooks

Minnesota and Other Poems, poetry by Daniel N. Nelson

Interviews from the Last Days, sci-fi poetry by Christina Loraine

the oneness of Reality, poetry by Brock Mehler

ABOUT THE AUTHOR

Patrick Cabello Hansel is the author of the poetry collection *The Devouring Land* (Main Street Rag Publishing) and the novella *Searching*, serialized in 33 issues of *The Alley News.* He has published poems and prose in over 65 journals, including *Crannog, Ilanot Review, Ash & Bones, Pirene's Fountain* and *Lunch Ticket.* He has been nominated for a Pushcart Prize and received awards from the Loft Literary Center and the MN State Arts Board. He is a recently retired Lutheran pastor, having served over 35 years in bilingual parishes in the Bronx, Philadelphia and Minneapolis. He lives in Minneapolis with his wife Luisa, a pastor and visual artist, and close to his two adult daughters, Natasha and Talia.